THERE ARE NO MULLIGANS!

Wootten House Publishing
Redwood City, CA 94061
November, 2010
www.therearenomulligans.com
info@therearenomulligans.com

ISBN 13: 978-0-9831063-0-2

The stories in this book are to the best of my memory.
My lack of memory, however, is legendary, so this book
may be more fictional than intended.

Cover Design by Michelle:
Sunshine11@sbcglobal.net

Printed by Allura Printing, Inc.
Rene Gagnon, CEO
Costa Mesa, CA
www.alluraprinting.com
rene.gagnon@alluraprinting.com

It is my intent for all net proceeds from this book to be
donated to Autism Speaks, California Autism
Foundation, PFLAG, One Box For Hope, Inc., and The
Diabetes Foundation; all great charities.

ii

BIO

Dennis J. Wootten is a native San Franciscan and a product of Catholic education. He received his BS in Accounting from the University of San Francisco in 1970 and his MBA in Accounting from Golden Gate University in 1976.

From 1967 through 1995, Mr. Wootten's career focus was finance and accounting. He held positions with banks, mortgage companies and a REIT.

In 1995, Mr. Wootten and his current business partner formed John Parry & Alexander a Human Resource and Administrative Services consulting firm. Over the next 14 years JPA worked with a wide variety of community banks and non-profit companies.

In July 2007, JPA was sold, and after fulfilling a short employment agreement, he and his business partner formed EW Partners, Inc., a HR consulting firm.

Mr. Wootten has been a member of the San Francisco's Mayor's Fiscal Advisory Board. He has also served on the Board of Catholic Charities, CFO of United Way of Santa Clara and is a Board member of California Autism Foundation.

He holds an active California Real Estate Broker's License and is licensed for all forms of insurance (California).

Mr. Wootten lives in Redwood City, California, with his wife of 40+ years. He enjoys golfing (poorly), reading, and an active family life with his three sons and two grandchildren.

DEDICATION

Thank you to my wife and best friend for all her years of patience and love. This book was written to pass some of my experience on to my three sons, who make me so proud and my grandchildren whom I love so much.

FOREWORD

There are no mulligans in life. Decisions regarding your career, your family, and your reputation become part of the permanent record. There are no opportunities to have a "do over". All the more reason to make sure you get sound advice as you face critical decisions. Are you tired of getting advice from so called experts? You know the ones I'm talking about; the doctors without children but who are quick to give advice on how to raise them and the priest who counsels you on martial relationships and sexual situations. Experts often have a string of letters after their names but no practical experience.

I thought it may be about time for advice from someone who is "just a regular guy". Someone whose basis for giving advice is simple; I am old and have lived through a lot of it.

This book is nothing more than a sharing of my experiences, good and bad, and how looking back I might have done things differently. In some cases, maybe most, I was lucky that things worked out for the best. Certainly, that is the case with my marriage. At printing, we are starting year 42 of married life. Although that fact may more be a statement on my wife's endurance levels than anything I've done correctly.

Worst case, maybe this book is something you can hand your son or daughter when they won't listen to you and say, "Here, read what this old guy says".

Enjoy reading about my life experiences.

TABLE OF CONTENTS

HUMBLE BEGINNINGS

Humble Beginnings

It wasn't until the fourth draft of this book that I decided to add a chapter on my early life. I think I have always "blocked" a lot of these memories out of my mind. However, I owe it to my grandchildren to let them know how everything started and how it may have influenced my development. I should have my younger brother write this chapter since he remembers so much more than I do. Sometimes I wonder if I was really there at all.

We grew up in the Noe Valley area of the Mission District of San Francisco. This was before the entire area became "trendy" and saw a major facelift. If I had to rank the area economically, I would guess it to be lower middle class. Initially, we lived in a flat that my parents rented. Later, my father would inherit a flat, a few blocks away, from his cousin that was like an aunt to him. I remember there was some family turmoil about her decision. My father owned a bar in the Tenderloin area of San Francisco on Geary Street; a few blocks west of the Theatre District. This was not an "upscale" establishment. The clientele were almost exclusively regulars; blue collar workers, merchant seamen and the like. There was a jukebox that played 45's (I used to love getting the records after my father changed them out every few months). Mostly, the customers were there all day and all night. They even cashed their paychecks at the bar. I never knew how my father did financially, but I think it was modest. My mother really never worked, other than a very brief stint as a LVN very late in her short life.

My brother and I both went to St. Philip's Catholic Elementary School. The early years seemed good.
I remember my mom being a Cub Scout den mother and working at the church festival. She was a good cook. I loved the beef stew, split pea soup and her meat sauce. I can remember my Dad bringing me the latest marvel comic books whenever I was sick. I was involved in Cub Scouts, Boy Scouts, traffic patrol, basketball (had to, I was the tallest in my class) and, of course, the mandatory altar boy service. I still remember the May Crowning ceremony for the Virgin Mary where I accidentally set the altar carpet on fire with the incense burner. I think the nuns would have killed me that day if they could have caught me.

My brother and I were constantly playing outside, from early morning until dinner or later. The only exception would be when it rained and we played board games or poker with the neighbors (my mom taught all the neighborhood kids to play poker; she always found a way to lose to us).

One thing my parents did that was critical to how we developed was they insisted on us having a Catholic education. We went to Catholic elementary school, Catholic high school (Sacred Heart), and I went to the University of San Francisco (first in the family to go to college). At the very least we received an excellent education and acquired discipline in our lives.

In the summers, my mother, brother and I would go to either Clearlake (early years) or Russian River (later years) for the entire summer. My father would come up on Friday nights. We didn't have a summer home; we rented a cabin and eventually had a small trailer. Again, my brother and I just roamed around all day and all night on our own. Great freedom!

I was happiest on that occasional Saturday when my father would take my brother and I to the all day cartoon movies at a theater on Market Street. My father would make a large bag of buttered popcorn with lots of salt and bring it to the movies. You could see and feel the grease coming through the brown bag. They would play Looney Tunes and Disney cartoons and at the break have a game of bingo for a bucket of silver dollars. We would follow that with lunch at Doggie Diner on Van Ness Avenue. A perfect day!

Here is a funny story where some future negotiation skills were uncovered. My parents were out for the day and my brother and I were home alone. We got into an argument that led to a physical fight. My brother got the worst of it and he had some bumps on his head and his face was all red. I was afraid that my parents would see him and know we had been fighting. I ordered my brother to take a bath and to soak his head to get the swelling down. My parents came home while he was in the tub in the middle of the day and knew something was wrong. They figured out quickly that we had been fighting. We had a long family meeting were I was able to convince my parents that we were fighting because we were frustrated. Our frustration was caused by us not having a large enough weekly allowance. My brother sat there listening with his mouth hanging open. My parents agreed to give us both an increase and we went on our way without any punishment. To this day my brother feels he got the bad end of the deal since he got the same increase but had to put up with a beating.

Somewhere in those early years something went wrong. My father and mother always smoked, a lot. Later after a TB scare, my father finally quit. My mother smoked three packs a day. Everything in the house was stained yellow from the smoke; the drapes, the curtains, the lampshades, her fingers and her teeth. Luckily, or because of it, my brother and I have never been smokers. Worse than that, however, was the alcohol abuse. My mother and father grew further and further apart.

The altercations between them grew more frequent and more violent. The abuse was both verbal and physical. My brother remembers me standing between my mother and father and me telling my father to "back off". He thinks I was about 10 years old at the time. I have no recollection of it.

My brother and I spent more and more time outside. Basketball, street baseball, touch football and stair baseball consumed all our time. Our neighbor's house is where we spent time indoors. We did anything to stay away from the environment in our home.

One time we were hanging around the neighborhood and we had found an old spare tire in the street. My brother either decided or was convinced it would be fun to roll it down the steepest hill in the neighborhood. It was on 22ndStreet and we called it the step hill, because the sidewalks were actually concrete steps for

6

the entire block. He rolled the tire down the steps and unbelievably enough it went down the entire hill. It reached the bottom right when a woman walked into its path and it knocked her down. We took off. Later that day I told my brother that the woman had died and that the police were looking for him. I told him the best place to hide would be the abandoned pigeon coop in the backyard. After he spent an entire night in the coop I told him that everything was ok, it had been a joke. He wasn't happy about that.

The good news is that we somehow avoided substance abuse problems as adults. I developed friends from the neighborhood that I still stay in touch with today. I think it also created in me the need to make and keep friends; they were my way of escaping.

My mother died of a heart attack at the age of 56 and my father of a stroke related condition at the age of 62. Even in those days it was considered young.

I'm just happy that it is all behind me.

SCHOOL YEARS

SCHOOL YEARS

When you are young you can't wait to get to the next level. From elementary school to high school, from freshman to senior, or on to college, we are always in a rush to move on. Sometimes the elementary and high school years are the worst. We always remember how tough and cruel our peers were. In that sense, it was great to be rid of all that stuff. It was nice to move on to the corporate world where no one says anything mean to you (just about you and behind your back). As an adult, one of the first lessons we learn is how good life was then. We really had few responsibilities.

The first mistake I made in elementary and high school was one of omission. I was insecure and didn't want to be rejected. The best way not to be rejected is not to take any risks. Don't participate in anything. Don't try out for athletic teams, debate, drama, class offices, music, even though the choices are many. Of course, that attitude then rolls over into girls and dating. You certainly don't want to risk rejection in this area, so stay shy and introverted, no matter what.

So, I didn't try out for teams. I did play basketball in elementary school because there was no fear of cuts. In fact, being 6'4" tall in 7th grade would have assured me a spot on the team anyway. I loved playing basketball. In fact, in my adult life I ended up playing until I was 50. After that I found that one week was not enough time for my body to heal from playing two hours of basketball. The cortisone shots, orthopedic supports, ankle taping, knee brace and elbow support was becoming a little "over the top" for someone of my very limited skill level.

Of course drama, debate or anything of that nature was absolutely out of the question. Imagine being up there in front of everyone, exposed to unlimited ridicule. Singing was not to be discussed. A nun in elementary school fixed that when she had told me to "mouth" the words in choir since I was a monotone. It wasn't until I got home did I find out from the dictionary that being classified a monotone was not a good thing.

Dating was a concept of terror. Talking to a girl was tough enough. Asking one out was pure torture. So, true to form, I didn't go to my high school proms. (Looking back, the fact I ever got married is nothing short of a miracle or some high degree of insight by my wife in thinking this guy might work out in the long run).

Then you finally get free of the school system and all that competition. Yeah, right, everyone knows there is no competition in the real world of finding a job, developing a career, raising a family and making it to retirement with something more than "two nickels to rub together".

The lesson here is that I wasted a lot of opportunities in those early years. Experiences that would have built up my confidence earlier and more fully were avoided. Trying and failing or even better, succeeding, are important experiences to prepare us for life. I look back and think, yeah, I could have made that high school basketball team, not started, but made the team. I probably could have found someone to go to a prom with. I now know there were girls with the same insecurities that I suffered, that would have loved to have someone ask them. Even that "skinny, string bean" might have been considered.

As for competition, most of the people that know me now would say that I am very competitive, not to mention, very outgoing. A trait that, at this point, I know is a good thing, not something to avoid.

Please try everything. Put yourself out there. Take chances. My experience is that most of us have a much lower opinion of ourselves than those around us have. If you have children, force them to try out for things. Yes, harass them until they do it.

MARRIAGE

MARRIAGE

Do I dare write anything about my marriage? I must have a death wish!

Luckily, in my case this is not a mistake I'm discussing, but a success. If there was a mistake, it was the age that my wife and I married. We were very young, even by the standard of those days. I was 20 and she was 19. I still had my senior year of college to complete, albeit, only 20 units for the year. I was working part-time for Wells Fargo Bank and she was working full-time in Retail Sales. She was from a solid Italian family with a strong work ethic, loving parents with overwhelming generosity, especially for this non-Italian who was in love with their daughter. I'm not sure if they ever really felt it would work out, but it did. This year we are celebrating our 42nd anniversary, although, at this point, the celebrations tend to be pretty low key.

How did I do it? To be honest, I was very lucky. She was a beautiful woman and still is to this day, looking much younger than her years. But that wasn't the lucky part. The lucky part was that she saw something in me that she believed she could meld, grow with, and train to be someone that we both could be proud of. I don't think she has changed much and really didn't need to. She definitely developed me into a decent father.

However, her efforts were not limited to my development. She was an equal partner in this marriage and played a key role. Of course, she managed the household and most of the children issues. Not the least of which was a great home cooked meal every night where we would all meet together no matter how many directions we were all flying off to (more on the child raising efforts later), and an organized, clean home. I think more importantly we complemented each other very well. She toned me down. I was the more aggressive one on my career changes, investing and spending money. She was able to bring a more cautious and conservative influence, which in most cases, proved to be needed. I had to do my homework so that I could convince her that certain decisions would work out. It kept me focusing on the risks as well as the rewards. Together we became a pretty good team. She gave me room on the financial side and I went with her decisions when it came to the needs of the children.

With all that love and flowers stuff aside, we would both agree that being married is mostly hard work. Getting through the fights, the hard economic times, and the general disappointments and tragedies that life throws at you. A couple of absolutes:

- When you argue, you don't leave the building. You stay and work it out, no matter what was said or you just stay silent.

- You try not to say those few secret things that you know will hurt your partner the most.

- You don't bring the parents into your disagreements, even if it is about them.

- You remember when thinking about leaving, the impact that it will have on your children and your extended family.

Throughout our marriage, my wife and I have rarely been apart for more than a few days at a time; usually my short business trips or my annual houseboat trip. One year though my wife and oldest son took a trip to Hawaii without me. I think I had to work. I remember thinking, "Now I can do everything I want. I can eat what I want, read at the table, watch whatever I want on TV and go to the gory movies". I was in Heaven for exactly one day before being bored out of my mind. Boy, I missed her that week.

Choose your partner carefully. It is the most critical decision you will make your entire life. That is why making the decision when you are a little older and have experienced living on your own might be a good thing. Although, I have seen many people wait until they are older and then find themselves too entrenched to change their ways for another person. They become resistant to change and too set in their life patterns. Don't avoid the commitment; just be ready to make a lot of sacrifices and changes. The good news is that it is worth it. You might find your best friend like I did.

HEALTH

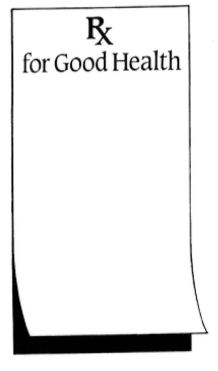

HEALTH

This section should have actually been the first in this book. It is not only the most important but also my worst mistake. All through my life I have had terrible eating habits. A high protein diet with lots of carbohydrates has been my usual fare. No fruit or vegetable intake whatsoever. Recently, Dr. Oz has stated that 70% of our health depends on how we live our life.

The results are not surprising. I developed Type II Diabetes in my fifties, had two heart stents inserted to avoid a heart attack, blood pressure problems, high cholesterol counts, and suffer from kidney stones. I currently take 19 pills every day. I have a disease called Chyluria which punishes me if my fat intake is anything but very modest.

I have just turned 62 and it is very difficult for this "old dog to learn a new trick". Eating habits are very hard to change.

My wife has often said that I will probably die of stupidity; doing something I know I shouldn't.

Here is a great story about that, although it strays somewhat from the topic of health.

I wanted to run some speaker wires from one side of the house to the backyard. We have a small crawl space under the house but it is not concreted; just dirt. I knew I would have to wait until my wife went to work because I would make a mess of myself and the house. So once she went to work I stripped down to my underwear (I didn't want to get my clothes dirty) and went underneath the house. This is not my favorite place as I constantly think about something crawling on me when I can't get out of the way. Initially, everything worked out as planned. I crawled to the opposite side of the house and dragged the wires with me. I successfully passed the wires through the vents. Everything was perfect! I started back to the opening to get out and had to pass under an air conditioning duct. I got stuck. I was lying on my stomach and couldn't move forward. I was in a panic! What if a rat or huge spider came at me? He wouldn't have to eat me to kill me; just walking over me would give me a heart attack. So now I'm thinking; I'm not getting out of here for hours until my wife comes home and calls the fire department to pull me out. Then I'll get to explain why I am just in my underwear. I was finally able to turn over onto my back and used the floor joists to leverage myself enough to finally pull myself through.

I think that men are basically DUMB! We always wait too long before seeking medical attention. I did this when I first started having symptoms of diabetes and again with angina (heart problems). I ignored angina pains, cold sweats, and the inability to walk just a few blocks. I even decided to drive myself to an emergency room, an hour away, so I could be closer to home. Considering the above, it is a miracle I am still alive!

24

Some moderate changes in my early years could sure have made things a lot better now. Please listen to those who tell you not to smoke (one habit I did avoid), to reduce your alcohol intake, and cut back on those heavy carbohydrate meals. Start with some sort of exercise program early and stay with it. Find the one time during the day where you will consistently make the time to exercise.

One of the things that helps relieve stress is to find a way to relax every day. For me the best way is to read. I read in the bathroom, when I eat by myself, and definitely, while waiting in the doctor's office. I have even encouraged two of my sons and a number of friends to start reading. I usually ask them, "Just read one book that I will give you". I always give them a book by Clive Cussler, one of my favorite authors. His books have lots of action and humorous dialogue. Invariably, they become avid readers for pleasure. Every night, while watching TV, you will find me "On my perch", as my wife calls my favorite chair, reading my Kindle. Try it, you'll find a whole new world.

Don't have an old body early in your life. You want to be able to enjoy the later years when you finally have some disposable income and the time to travel and do the things you like to do.

Do your families a favor, EAT HEALTHLY, EXERCISE, AND VISIT YOUR DOCTOR!

CHILDREN

CHILDREN

Nothing is more challenging and rewarding than children. What a responsibility and a thrill. It would be so much better if you could have them when you are 50 years old and have the patience (more on this) and experience you need to handle this job. There is no training to go thru, you just do it by instinct and you don't get a "mulligan".

When they are infants (we had twin sons and an older son, all within three years of age), the workload is unbelievable! You are changing diapers and doing feedings almost constantly. You are always angry because you think you are doing the most work. You feel your partner must not be doing enough since you are always exhausted. The truth is that three young children do require a "village" not just two adults. You have no time for yourselves. No movies, no dinners out, or vacations for at least a couple of years. Thank God for my wife's family, without their considerable help, we would have never gotten to go out. My wife wanted a night out for dinner and a movie. We stood in line around the block to see the movie "Jaws" (yes, the first one). This is a movie that unless she was desperate there was "no way" she would ever agree to see something so gory and terrifying.

But eventually children do grow up and the problems you face change. They don't get any easier, they just change. Cruel peers at school, teachers who have no interpersonal skills at all because they have the "power", competition in sports, teenage years, learning how to drive, choosing college, it just all wears you down. During each phase you think the next level will be easier. Not true, it never is, and we have good kids (actually, we have GREAT kids).

Have you ever asked your son or daughter if they had finished something you asked them to do and get the answer "I didn't have enough time!" This always made me crazy! I would tell them, "No problem, I'll find the time for you. When I left for work at 5AM, you were sleeping; when I came home, you were watching television; after dinner when I started working again, you were playing video games; when I went to bed at 11:30PM, you had been asleep for an hour already. So, tomorrow I will wake you at 5AM when I get up so you'll "find the time you need to do what I had asked". Almost without exception they found the time themselves.

This can be a two way street though. Sometimes I don't listen to what I am saying. A friend of mine took my three sons and I waterskiing. We had never been before, so he was going to teach us all. This is a very patient guy. Before we got to the lake I told my sons, repeatedly, that if they should fall that they have to let go of the rope immediately! I didn't want them to get dragged thru the water. When we got on the boat I told them again. When each son went into the water they were told a third time. Everybody performed well and
30

remembered my instructions. It was now my turn. I had never gotten up on skis and this time was no different. I tried but kept falling quickly. You can guess what happens next, can't you? When I fell I would continue to hold onto to the rope and try to get my legs back in the front of me while under water and being pulled by a ski boat. Yeah, that is going to happen. My sons all got the last laugh and asked me "Dad, what are you supposed to do when you fall? LET GO OF THE ROPE! " Yes, sometimes fathers don't take their own advice.

We did, however, do some things right:

- Catholic schools (yeah, I know the public schools are good too).

- We instilled a belief that if you work hard you will out perform other students who are more intelligent.

- I tried to be home every night for dinner with the family and to help with homework. Limit your overtime. Occasionally, I would go back to work late at night when everyone else was in bed.

- My wife was constantly involved with them with doctor appointments and twice weekly allergy shots. She drove car pool, she worked the hot lunch program, drove them to their games and activities, helped with the homework and school projects, and made sure we ate as a family every night. What this did was kept them under her observation for most of the day when they weren't actually in school. This is critical to making sure they are not getting into the wrong crowd or just "hanging" around too much. The most critical part was that she fought to make sure they received any special help they might need whether at the school or an outside resource. This early help certainly paid dividends when they went on to high school and college.

- I coached their elementary school basketball teams. We seldom won, but we had fun and it kept me involved with them after school and on Saturdays.

- Making college attendance something that was rarely discussed; it was assumed they would all go. Only the college selection was up for discussion.

- Manage their high school and college class selections, even when they "don't need the help".

- During the high school years, making sure they were kept busy with plenty of extracurricular activities; no time to just "hang around". We encouraged them to have part time jobs. They all rose to the challenge, whether it was in banking, scooping ice cream or in retail. They worked hard and they took it seriously.

- Not letting smoking take a hold in any of the kids.

- Keeping a watchful eye on underage drinking; there is always going to be some.

- If you are going to drive or own a car you WILL have a job to help pay the costs. I insisted they do a budget showing their costs and their income. That is when they learned that you have to plan income on a net basis not a pretax basis. This ended up being a valuable skill for them. It doesn't matter that I can afford for you not to work. You appreciate and take care of things you have to pay for.

- It was understood, If you decide not to go to college, you WILL have a job if you expect to stay at home.

- You can take as long as you want to finish your college education. You should enjoy those years. However, just remember, we are only going to pay for four years. The rest of the time will be on you.

- Be persistent. If you ask a question and the answer is NO. It doesn't mean NO; it means you haven't asked the question the right way.

A short story on that:

My twin sons both applied and got accepted to the University of San Francisco, my alma mater. They both received a small academic scholarship. One twin decided to go to UC Santa Barbara instead. I told the family I was going to call USF and see if the academic scholarship for the twin not attending could be added to the scholarship for the one who had decided to attend. The family laughed and told me I was absolutely crazy.

I called and the money was transferred over. Key lesson; it never hurts to ask.

My twin going to UCSB was majoring in Education. A class he needed as a prerequisite was impacted. He called and asked me what to do. I told him to attend the class (crash the course). He did and called the next day and said the teacher advised all those trying to "crash" his course to forget about it. He never allows any late enrollments. I told him to keep going for at least two or three weeks and to make sure he participated in class. He did just that and one day the teacher asked him to stay after class. He told my son that he was going to allow him to enroll in the class since if he wasn't around there wouldn't be anyone participating.

SIMPLY, BE RERSPECTFULLY PERSISTENT.

Things I did wrong (note I said "I" and not "we", my wife was much better than I):

- No Patience. I'm doing a chapter on this. I was easy to anger and just was not very patient. To this day, I regret that I wasn't more patient with my children. They deserved much better.

- Excessive verbal yelling and swearing was a real easy habit to fall into. It set a very intimidating environment for them, and it is immature.

- Not being encouraging enough in them. I all too often would say I wanted them to do better rather than celebrating what they had already accomplished.

OK, it was a much shorter list, and I'm sure when I let my sons read this book they will come up with many more items to include. However, to my way of thinking, it was too long already.

When I think back, I remember telling my wife, "I just wanted a dog".

THE CRASH BROTHERS

THE CRASH BROTHERS

The worst thing about raising children, the most horrific and the most stressful is not the first day of school, it is not the wedding day, it is what every parent fears the most; teaching your teenage child how to drive.

When we have driven for a while we have a change in our focus. We pay as much attention to those cars two or three cars ahead of us as the one in front of us. We can sense when a car is going to move into our lane, before they use their turn signal or even turn their head. We sense it.

The teenage driver focuses almost entirely on the car in front of them and on the actual physical act of driving. Of course, this leads to them getting into a few "fender benders" and receiving a few tickets for speeding or illegal maneuvers from our local police.

What can be done to eliminate this period of exposure? Not a damn thing!

It is like learning how to use the internet or your first video game. It just takes hours and hours of practice. No amount of instruction or yelling will shorten this learning period.

My twins struggled with this period. They started driving while in high school like most teens and their high school campus was the site of quite a few accidents. They hit a parked car while leaving school. They were hit when they came out of the parking lot. Their car was hit by a baseball while parked in the lot. If there was a way to have an accident; they found it.

There was always the proclamation that, "It wasn't my fault!" The insurance company usually thought otherwise.

So, it is not surprising that their school mates would give them a nick name. They became known as "The Crash Brothers".

I remember one such incident, away from the campus. My son, the EMT, was driving on 101 heading toward San Francisco. The streets were wet after a recent rain. He rear ended someone and was upset. He had done all the right things; offered medical treatment, offered to call the paramedics, offered to call the police, but the other driver insisted that he was fine and they traded insurance information.

He took the closest exit off the freeway and called me. "Dad, I've been in an accident and my car is leaking some kind of fluid. Can you come and check it out?"

I went to meet him and his car was damaged, but was drivable. The leaking fluid looked to be coolant. I called a very good friend who owns a body shop in Oakland. He told me, "Den, if the car is drivable then just bring the car in so we can check it out. Just have your son follow you over to the shop so you can drive him home". I told him, "He just rear ended someone I don't want him following ME anywhere!"

The best advice during this period of time is to buy cheap cars. Don't run out to get that brand new sports or muscle car for your son or daughter. They will have an accident. Wait until they have two years of driving experience before you ever think to upgrade the vehicle.

So we fast forward now to the present. My twins are in a fantasy football league with my friends and I. They have to have a name for their team.

Yes, it is "THE CRASH BROTHERS".

PARENTS SEEM TO KNOW

PARENTS SEEM TO KNOW

Sometimes parents just seem to know.

They can see things their children just don't focus on. They can pierce those little white lies. They know when something isn't quite right.

I have a few stories that prove this point.

My wife and I had a Ford Country Squire station wagon. This is the old style wagon that could fit a small house inside it. It had the "fake" wood siding and the tilt up third seat; a real classic.

We had lent the car to one of our twin sons. He was going to go out with some friends. The next day I was putting something into the back of the car and noticed there was a long crack in the interior plastic side panel that wasn't there before. I called my son down to the car and asked him, "What happened to the car?" He said, "Gee, I don't know Dad, I think it must have been there before".

I said, "You know, it looks like damage you would get if a keg of beer was rolling around in the back of the car and smashed into the side".

"Who told you?"

"No one, son, but now with your reaction I know my wild guess was right. I think we need to have a little talk about this".

The next story is even better.

My oldest son was in college and my wife and I and our other sons were going out of town for the weekend. We had decided to let my oldest son stay at home. He was old enough and, of course, we laid out a lot of rules. My son decided to throw a party. He planned it out very well. He took Polaroid pictures of each room and the placement of all the furniture. He then had his friends help him move all the furniture out of the rooms into the garage; including the pictures on the walls. He had the perfect plan.

When we arrived home from our weekend away, we entered the house thru the garage into the downstairs family room, as was our habit. My wife took one step into the family room and declared, "Something is not right here!" She knew right away that things had been moved, I think she also spotted a peanut behind the couch in the family room. As we started checking things out in more detail, I found a couple of beer bottles behind the shed in the backyard and she found some pictures not quite straight. We figured out that

46

our oldest son had a party in the house. We confronted him and eventually, after the first denials, confessed that he had had a party. I asked him, "Was it worth it?" He said, "It was the worse party ever! I was nervous the whole time, the police came about the noise, the party spilled out into the street, and I never got to enjoy myself. I worked like Hell moving the furniture back and forth and cleaned the entire house from top to bottom. I'm exhausted." I think we eventually even found a lemon peel on one of the blades on the kitchen fan.

Parents just seem to know!

CHARACTER

CHARACTER

How do you define character?

We speak of someone having character but what are the attributes that we assign to this all encompassing word?

Is it integrity, compassion for others, honesty, courage, generosity, wanting to change people's lives or living conditions, or respect?

Clearly it is a combination of traits. We have difficulty defining it but not much difficulty in knowing when we see it. I am very blessed to have three sons who have lots of character. Don't quite know how it happened or what directly caused it but happy to see it.

One of our twin sons is a Physician Assistant and works in the emergency room of a hospital. His road to this position was long. It started in high school. He was a shy student and really hadn't found anything that interested him a lot. He one day decided it would be fun to ride along with some EMT's (Emergency Medical Technician) and Paramedics. It was part of an Explorer program. He loved it and it changed his life. He became more and more involved. He ran for and won the Explorer Post President's position. Next, he told us he wanted to be an EMT. The requirements were that you had to be 18 years of age and a high school graduate. He had just finished his junior year in high school, but he was already 18 years old. He had figured a way that he wouldn't have to wait another year. He decided to take the High School Equivalency Exam and receive his degree a year early (although he would still continue thru high school and graduate with his class). So when he started his senior year in high school he had a part time job as an EMT. This was quite an accomplishment. It didn't stop there. He attended USF (University of San Francisco) as a pre-med student with hopes of becoming a doctor. During his college years he decided he wanted to become a Paramedic. He thought about leaving college to go into a paramedic program. I promised him if he stayed in college and graduated that I would pay for his paramedic studies. He graduated and completed his additional studies and became a paramedic.

I remember one evening at a USF basketball game a player took a fall and hit his head on the floor and just laid there. My son went down to assist and ended up "taking over the scene" giving advice to the trainer and the orthopedic doctor that was in attendance. He coordinated the efforts of the paramedics when they arrived and advised them of the injured player's condition and his efforts to that point. This was my shy, introverted son, "taking over the scene". I was amazed and proud!

He had always wanted to go to Medical School, but the cost and the length of time required was difficult to justify. Instead, now married at the time, he decided to become a PA (Physician Assistant) and continue his work in emergency medicine. He was accepted into a program in Indiana and moved there with his wife. This was a tough program but again he succeeded. He graduated with honors and came back to California. He found a job in Central California and is still working in emergency medicine. It is a difficult career, always dealing with people when they are in the worst situations. You have to have compassion and the ability to distance your self from the suffering; a trying combination of skills.

My other twin son also decided on his career choice very early. In his Junior or Senior year in high school he had decided he wanted to become a history teacher. He had taken some Advanced Placement courses in high school and was already earning some college credits. He had a number of universities that he had applied and was accepted to and we did a number of campus visits. He eventually decided on the University of California at Santa Barbara. He liked the idea of going away to college. The education program at the college was "impacted", meaning that certain courses were very hard to get into and so the program could take longer to complete. He took a position as a Resident Assistant to earn a little extra money. He worked hard and was able to graduate in four years. Next up were graduate studies to obtain his teaching credential and his master's degree. He attended USF for his master's degree program and was actually already teaching in an elementary school while he was working on the program. While he enjoyed teaching, he was really not interested in doing so at the elementary school level. His goal was to teach at the high school level. Eventually, after a number of schools and a good number of years, he was able to secure a position at a Catholic girl's high school. He started teaching religion and after numerous requests was finally allowed to do some History teaching.

He frequently puts in 10 hour days, deals with classes of teenage girls each day, and then helps with or attends school clubs, bowling, JSA, dances, retreats, school plays, games, or other school based activities. He takes the girls to Sacramento and Washington D. C. for Close Up to learn about government, He financially supports Breast Cancer Awareness, Save Darfur, Arthritis Foundation, Autism Speaks, California Autism Foundation, Mercy Beyond Borders, and the Assumption Sisters College Fund, just to name a few. He gives, yet, his summer is spent teaching in Summer School so he can make enough money to live.

This is not a profession that you choose because of the financial rewards. He wants to make these girls the best that they can be, prepare them for college and give them a great high school experience to look back on. It takes someone special to dedicate themselves to improving others.

For a long time, I thought teaching was an easy job. There are short hours, no stress to climb the corporate ladder, and three months vacation each summer. I had an opportunity to learn how wrong I was on this.

For nine years I volunteered one hour a week to teach in an eighth grade classroom. It was a program called Project Business and was a part of Junior Achievement. The program covered careers, basic economics (supply and demand), how to complete job applications, budgeting, and a stock market game. My time was volunteered by my employer. I thought "how tough can this be?"

Well the answer was VERY TOUGH. The kids were great; energetic, engaging and participative. However, it took five to six hours of preparation to have enough material for that one hour class. It was difficult to be engaging and interesting for a full hour. I'm very outgoing and I joke around a lot so I could keep most of the kids listening. Remember, I was only doing this for one hour a week. How could my son do this job six hours a day, five days a week?

I had a new respect for my son and all Teachers!

My oldest son's example of character is not career based; although he is very successful in his career. He amazed us on a decision he had made as a teen.

He was very popular in high school and went to a lot of dances and proms. He knew a lot of the girls at the local Catholic girl's high schools. One day I was in the hallway outside of his room when he received a call. He was talking to a girl from one of the above high schools. I overheard him say, "Yeah, I would love to go. We will have a lot of fun. I'll call you in a couple of weeks to work out the details. Thanks for asking me".

I asked him, "Another prom"?

"Yes, my friend Sydney has asked me to her prom".

Well, Sydney was a girl that had a very serious disability. She was about the size of a 3rd grader and her body was so physically challenged that she found it difficult to walk. In fact, most of the time, her classmates at school would actually carry her to class because of all the hills. She had never been to a dance and wanted my son to take her to her Senior Prom.

When my son went to pick her up for the dance, her parents had tears in their eyes because their daughter was so happy. At the dance, for the picture taking, she had to sit on his knee so their heads would be level for the shot. During the dance he would have to carry her while dancing. He focused on her having a great time at her first dance, and consequently, he did too.

We had so many parents call us after that event to tell us how amazing our son was. If you think back to when you were a teen, would you have made the same decision? I'm sure I wouldn't without first thinking about it a lot. His decision took a lot of courage. The funny thing was that he never even thought about it. It was automatic for him. He never saw her disability as something for him to consider.

Recently two of my nieces have set up their own charity. One niece is married to a man from Nicaragua and they go there to visit his family. On one of their trips my niece and her sister visited a school and they were touched by the needs of the school and the children. They decided to start a non-profit to provide charity and relief to the poor, distressed and under privileged residents of rural La Concepcion, Nicaragua, by providing clothing, school supplies and building materials. The name of the charity is One Box For Hope, Inc.

These are all great examples of real character!

DIVERSITY

DIVERSITY

I know this is a strange chapter for a Caucasian with a Caucasian wife. What would I know about diversity? The answer is not much and that is the point. I think I have always been pretty accepting and didn't see much bigotry in my life. Of course, self evaluations are always more gentle aren't they? However, I do have a major experience in my life that certainly made me think about it and regret how I had acted.

About nine years ago my oldest son took a job with an upscale department store in San Francisco selling women's handbags. Prior to that, he had always been very involved with fashion, always having the best clothes and just knowing what the "best of class" was in every clothing arena. He had a girlfriend for four and a half years, that he was very close to and they had seemed to be heading for a more serious commitment, when suddenly they broke up. I can remember "giving him a bad time" about the handbag job and asking him if he was gay. He kept telling me no and told me to leave him alone.

Shortly after that the whole family had gone out to see "Cats" and to dinner. At this time, my son was living in the Marina district of San Francisco and we drove him home. When he exited the car, he looked back in and told us "by the way, I am gay". We told him to get back in the car and we drove to a nearby bar to talk about it as a family. To their credit, his brothers were incredibly accepting, "no big thing, we had no idea, etc." My wife and I wanted to know if he had AIDS, does this mean you are a cross dresser, are you going to get a sex change operation? Just shows the level of our awareness. We all parted well and we did everything we could that day to let him know that we were accepting of him and that it certainly had no impact on how we felt about him.

We then went home and cried every night at dinner. No grandchildren at this time (he was the oldest son) and now a dismal outlook for the future. What will we do if he contracts AIDS? How terrible he must have felt all these years, especially through high school, when he must have known he was different.

We had to do something to educate ourselves and to get some support from people who have gone through this before us. My wife and I discussed how we would approach the subject with family and friends and decided we were not going to be ashamed of our son. We decided that we would tell everyone that our son is gay.

It was amazing when we told our family and friends how wrong we could be about some of the reactions. First, we thought we might get some negative comments and we were sure that there were certain people because of their jobs, religion, or personality that they would just not be able to accept it. We couldn't have been more wrong. The acceptance for our son, while not universal, was certainly more than we anticipated.

We needed to educate ourselves on the issue. My wife did some research and found an organization called PFLAG (Parents & Friends of Lesbians and Gays). They had monthly meetings close to where we lived and we decided to attend a meeting.

That first meeting was memorable. What an awakening! To start the evening we sat in a circle and introduced ourselves to everyone. To our left was a man about 35 years old who stood up and reminded everyone that last week was National Coming Out Week and that as "everyone" knew that was the time of the highest suicide rates among gays. He had lost one of his best friends to suicide. We thought we had already conjured up every negative about our son being gay. Now here we are being horrified about a new risk. We were crushed. Tears were rolling down our cheeks.

The group portion of the meeting ended and we broke up into smaller groups. The group leader asked me how we were doing. I told him "not good". I relayed to the group that my son told us he was gay two weeks ago, and that we had been crying about it every night. That we had told our friends and family about it and that we had found out about PFLAG. His reaction was astonishment; he couldn't believe that we had accomplished this much in just two weeks. He told us we could be the poster family for PFLAG. He explained that many gays are rejected by their families and that many families choose to keep it "confidential".

Since then we have read up on the subject. We now understand it is not a "life style" choice, but a definite part of who he is. Believe me, no one would choose to be gay just to get all the humiliation, rejection, verbal and physical abuse that is heaped upon them. We now try to help other families and friends who end up in our situation with as much support as we can.

The part that really shook me was how much I may have impacted my son. Did my actions lengthen the time he "stayed in the closet"? How much did those jokes I came home with and those snickering comments about gays hurt him? To this day, I am still ashamed of my comments about gays prior to my son "coming out".

Yeah, it was nice that we educated ourselves about "being gay" and that we did some of the right things when we found out. However, it would have been much nobler if I had had this awakening without this personal incentive.

The lesson here is just to try to remember that these types of jokes and comments can hurt people around you that you don't even realize may have a gay son or daughter or other family member. I still make the same mistake, however, hopefully a little less often.

Our son, by the way, is very successful in the fashion industry and we are as proud of him as our other sons. He has a partner of twelve years and lives in New York City. His partner is one of the kindest and easiest going people you will ever meet. We love that he is part of our family.

Each of my sons has developed into their own success stories.

GRANDCHILDREN & GRANDDOG

GRANDCHILDREN & GRANDDOG

Grandchildren are a true blessing from God. They are so loving and so happy to see you. It just fills your heart. Of course, you want to buy them everything they want and take them to all the best places. Nothing makes you feel as good as being able to give someone something that really lights them up.

However, there is a real challenge here. We as grandparents don't have the same influence we once had as parents. You eventually realize that this is not your second chance in parenting. Your child is now a parent and he will do what he thinks is right.

For me, Grandchildren represented a second chance in being more patient. I wanted to be the most patient and the most loving Nonno. The failures I had in being patient with my own sons was not going to happen this time. I was better this time but very far from what I wanted or expected.

In our case, there was an additional challenge. Both of our grandchildren have special needs. It hurts us to see these kids work so hard to develop skills that come easier to others. They have gone through intensive behavior therapy starting at the age of two, and it has brought good results. Financially, the therapies, extra specialists, and the never ending tests create a difficult financial burden for the family. There is never an end for the work load. Yet, the parents come up with ways to make their children's lives more fun. They provide the kids with opportunities to experience different things like horseback riding, swimming lessons, ballet, karate, and baseball. My grandchildren seem to enjoy every experience.

The autism rates over the last few years are "off the charts". Some sources cite rates of 1 in every 100 births. This should just be unacceptable. The eventual economic impact of having this many autistic individuals in our society will be staggering. Find an organization in your area and support it financially and with your efforts. It is worthwhile.

This, however, has rallied our entire family. We have made it a family event to support the Annual Autism Walk and we have raised a significant amount for the sponsor, Autism Speaks. Recently, I have joined the Board of Directors of a fantastic organization, the California Autism Foundation. This is an organization that delivers services to children and adults with autism. It is so heart warming to see your family and friends step forward and donate both their time and money to help your cause.

You just don't know how much these children are absorbing. With my grandson, I would remind him to use his fork. He would get frustrated with me at times. The last time this happened we were at Disneyland, and we were having lunch at an Italian restaurant in the California Adventure Park. My grandson had pasta with chicken. Toward the end of the meal, I reached over and took a piece of chicken from his bowl. He said loudly and clearly, "Nonno use a fork!" I was ecstatic that he not only got it, but he was able to put me in my place. It was the best.

We are optimistic for both of our grandchildren. We know they are getting the best care, training and attention available. We are thrilled when their advances or surprises come about. A while ago, my grandson looked at a picture of a Disney character and told his mom, "I want to go to Disneyland with Nonno and Nonni ". She put them both on the phone and they repeated this to us and asked us if we would go. Of course, we couldn't turn down an invitation like that.

We just had another great experience, Grandparents Day at school. It started with me getting a call from my granddaughter, "Nonno, will you come to my school and to my class. Please! I really want you to come." I said, "Of course I will, when should I come?" She said, "right now Nonno, right now". Her mother whispered in the background, "No, tell him it is on Wednesday". We had a great time visiting both of their classrooms. Our grandson was so glad to see us and he did something so mature. When we entered the class he introduced us to his teacher and then to his aide. "Al (the aide), this is my Nonni and this is my Nonno (patting my stomach of good size)." This was the first time we saw him make an introduction. It was another example of his progression and also how happy he was.

There are great moments. My granddaughter had one I won't forget for quite a while. People with autism have problems with subtle humor since they generally can't read facial expressions well and they do not understand plays on words. One night while we were all out for dinner, my granddaughter turned to me and asked, "Nonno, What do crocodiles eat?" She likes crocodiles because of the character in Peter Pan. We had taken them to a live theatre performance of the classic and they loved it. I told her, "I think they like little blonde hair girls the most." She had a concerned look on her face and then she turned to me and said, "I think they like big people with no hair, and green eyes, named Nonno!" It was great for her to give back as good as she got. I loved it!

One summer we invited my son, his wife and the grandchildren to our timeshare in Maui. We had a lot of apprehension on how they would do with the flight over there with it being over five hours long. Also, they aren't used to spending that much time away from their own home and its comfort zones. My daughter-in-law decided to bring the car seats for them to use on the plane. I thought that was a lot to carry on the plane. She was right! They did great on the flight. They felt comfortable and secure in their own seats. We had a two bedroom timeshare with an ocean view. Marriott had been kind enough to child proof most of the doors before our arrival. My granddaughter's first reaction was that she wanted to go home. However, we had a great time in Maui. They played on a pirate ship in the children's pool. My grandson loves pirates. They danced in the aisles at the luau. We rode the sugar cane train. They swam every day. They enjoyed the trip and they adjusted to a new environment. When it was finally time to leave, my granddaughter who on the first day wanted to go home said she wanted to stay and live there. Don't we all?

A friend who was kind enough to edit an early draft of this book said "You have to include something about Oscar!" He was right. Oscar is our granddog; a lovely

Dachshund with a real attitude. A few years ago we decided to get our oldest son, who lives in New York City, a dog. My son and his partner have a fast pace existence. He has a high stress job in the fashion industry and his partner is running a retail pet store. We felt a dog could be a real solace and calming for both of them.

We found a breeder in Granite Bay, a small community a little north of Sacramento. They had an ad for a dachshund puppy and I had phoned about it. There was only one puppy left to adopt. I decided to take a trip up and see the dog, and if satisfied commit to the purchase. When I walked in I was stunned. There had to be 15 puppies and probably 6-8 adult dogs. The place was well kept and had a nice area for the dogs both inside and outside. I was pleased that they all seemed well cared for. I sat on the sofa and was immediately swamped by all of the dogs. They were climbing over me and each other. They were so happy to see me. I was like the little boy, in the commercial laughing, with all the dogs trying to lick him. I was laughing and telling my wife on the phone that this was the most fun I had had in a long time. It wasn't long before all of the dogs were exhausted and sleeping cuddled up to each other. What a sight!

I was sold. I bought the dog. We had to wait a number of weeks before we could actually take him home. He had to reach a certain age.

When we returned to take him home my son was with me. We got him in the car for the long two and a half hour ride home. My son was holding his dog and the poor little guy was shivering with fear. He had been taken from his mother and he was afraid of all this change. As soon as we got him home, we did everything we could to make him feel secure and loved.

Of course, now he is a member of the family. He travels to the West Coast with my son on visits, first class, of course, and we prepare for his arrival. We turn on the fireplace for him since he likes the warmth and he is treated like royalty.

His "Uncle Al", my son's cousin, also welcomes him to his home and cares for him; making sure he gets his favorite treats and some pancakes in the morning. The best is that Uncle Al always gives Oscar a nice bath with, of course, heated towels. All humor aside, he is a blessing and he is like a child to my son and his partner.

Little dog, big attitude, huge impact.

If there is reincarnation, come back as a dog!

PATIENCE

PATIENCE

I don't think there is a better attribute to try to develop. If you ask 100 people if they think they are patient, probably 100 will say they are very patient. For years, I would always say I am the most patient person around. Even to the point of arguing with my wife that "I AM TOO PATIENT!" Pretty obvious if you are yelling and arguing that you are patient, you have already lost the argument.

I look back with regret on the frequency which I lost my patience with my children and my wife. I so wish I had those years back. I keep seeing the faces of my twins when they were crushed by my show of disappointment with something that they did. It is so easy to let work and family stress trigger your temper.

My grown sons just recently reminded me about something. They said they were always careful to go to Mom's side of the bed in the middle of the night when they woke up sick. They knew not to wake me up since I would get angry. Not how you want to be remembered.

But it doesn't stop there, does it? No, you carry it to work, to the golf course (more on this soon), and wherever you go.

My son has two children with autism. The patience required is unbelievable! I am embarrassed when I see what he has to deal with and how relatively easy I had it and couldn't meet the requirements. Even as a grandparent it is difficult to be patient enough.

With measured patience you can increase your effectiveness as a manager, husband and, most importantly, a father. Work at it, walk away from potential arguments. Try to deliver your points through effective debate, or even better, through example.

If you can become more patient, you can enhance the quality of your life and your relationships. Avoid this serious character flaw. I didn't; but you can.

I remember reading a great phrase in the most recent Stephen King book, "Under the Dome". "Control your temper or it will control you". How true!

THE "SECRET"

THE "SECRET"

There was a book being discussed on the Oprah show one afternoon called "The Secret". My wife likes the show and had it on. OK, OK I also enjoy her show. The book has a huge following and is basically about the benefits of positive thinking. It explains that you can bring about certain things in life by simply focusing on them. This supposedly creates some type of positive energy that will actually make your dreams for success, health or wealth come true.

I'm a logical, process type guy, so this philosophy does not get a lot of traction with me. However, I had one thing in my life that I really wanted. I have two grandchildren. The little boy is the oldest and was about four at the time. My Grandson was also pretty much non-verbal at that time (thankfully he now is very much improved). He said some words but not very many sentences. This wasn't from a lack of desire. He would come up to me and go on a long monologue about something that he really wanted to tell me. With wide eyes and a lot of expression he struggled to try to communicate with me. I would sometimes not get it all. Whenever our visit with him would end, I would hold up my right hand like it was a phone and tell him "Call me sometime".

I decided that I would try out "The Secret", and focus on my grandson calling me on the phone. Every night in bed I would lay there and just try to mentally send him a message to pick up the phone and call me. Of course, I did this for months and nothing happened. I did not share this with my son or his wife. I didn't want them to just make it happen. I wanted it to be my grandson deciding he wanted to talk to his Nonno.

Then one day a miracle happened. I was at work and the phone rang. I answered with my usual greeting. This little voice answered, "Nonno, this is TJ". I was shocked and listened to him tell me a few things. After we finished, his mother came on the phone and explained that he was playing and he had his thumb and pinkie up to his ear and mouth pretending he was making a call and talking. She had asked him who he was calling and he answered, "Nonno". She then said, "Here, let me dial the real phone for you". This was a special gift this day since earlier that morning I had watched a close friend of mine pass away from cancer. This lifted me up!

Looking at the big picture, I know this is not a world stopping event. The author of "The Secret" will not be using this as another example of her philosophy at work. However, for me it was proof that sometimes positive thinking and focus will get you to where you need to go. We spend a lot of our time just running to the next task. Maybe some time is well used in thinking about what we want out of life, what things or issues really are important to us. In this case, my frequently telling him to call me planted the thought in his head about doing just that one day. The real lesson here is that it doesn't matter what the cause. What is important is doing some prioritization in your life and working toward what you want.

BALANCING YOUR TIME

BALANCING YOUR TIME

As you move up the ladder of corporate life, one thing is a certainty. You will be required to work harder and longer. You will put pressure on yourself to get to work before your boss and leave later than he does. You don't want him to think you aren't willing to work as hard as he does. There will always be more to do than you can do in a single day. There is always that one last thing you want to get done before you head home. If you are single, other than the stress you are putting onto yourself, you are doing no one any harm. If you are married and have a family, you are certainly impacting others. It is easy to miss dinner with the kids, find out they all went to bed before you got home, and then you go to your home office and do even more work. This makes for a great relationship with your wife too. She may have a job as well but she has to get home to feed everyone, help the kids with the homework and get them to bed while you are still at work.

First off, you need to have some confidence in your abilities to get things done and to do them right. Most managers, especially in today's telecommuting environments, are not being managed on the number of hours they work, but on the results they produce.

I took a little different approach. I rarely stayed late at work. I was home for dinner with my family just about every night. I was able to help my sons with their homework, at least until they got into the fifth grade when my knowledge was being surpassed. If I had more work to do I would do it when the rest of the family was sleeping. I did it on my own time rather than taking it away from my family time. I even occasionally drove back to work late at night, worked there, came home late, and then got up early and started all over. While taxing at times, I think it was the right way to do things. It was the fair way for the family. I think my wife appreciated it.

Balancing your time is also about giving to others. Participate in charities that you are interested in. Find time for your children's school and sports events. Coach their teams or volunteer for the parent's council at school or church. Use your management tools and experience to make organizations you care about more efficient. This is all worthwhile but be careful that this participation doesn't take away too much time from your family life. Remember this is not a substitute for working late.

Take a vacation every year and try to put two weeks together when you can. You'll find it almost takes a full week away before you stop checking your emails every hour and before you are actually willing to turn the cell phone off. You will also be surprised to find that you are replaceable. The entire world and your business struggled through nicely when you were gone. This is a reminder that anyone can be replaced. Yes, even you and me.

DRINKING

DRINKING

We often equate age with maturity. We say to our kids that when you grow up you'll understand and you will make better decisions. I'm not so sure this is true.

I recently had a 60th birthday party. It was a wonderful day and a beautiful party planned by my wife and looked forward to by both my family and friends. I did the smart thing and hired a driver to make sure I was not tempted to drink and drive. You would think that at sixty years old I would be mature enough to control my drinking. I certainly was old enough. Well, I got so intoxicated that I missed the end of my own party and wound up in the emergency room of the nearby hospital. I am a diabetic and have a heart condition so I had to be checked extensively to make sure these diseases were not in play.

My wife was, understandably, worried that I was dying. My sons were upset. I was out for four hours. My friends were worried that something terrible had happened.

It is easy to decide to drink less after a bad hang over. The physical discomfort is so severe you just know you do not want to be like that again. This resolution only lasts a few weeks.

When I look back over the years, I never thought I had any kind of drinking problem. Even with parents and uncles that clearly did. I always thought I controlled it pretty well. Now when I look back, I think of the times that I certainly should not have driven home but did anyway. I never got a DUI, but there were certainly times when I could have. Incidentally, I've been told that a DUI violation can cost you a couple of days in jail and $20,000 to $30,000 to defend. Plus you will experience a significant increase in insurance rates for at least five years.

I now understand there is even a higher cost; it is the shame that results. The pain you cause your family is significant. You have been diminished in the view of your friends, a reputation that you have built over many years.

So when you are tempted, don't control your drinking because of the physical pain or financial toll that might be inflicted. Control yourself because you don't want to harm your loved ones and because you do not want to reduce your presence, your esteem.

I know it will be my incentive and I will try to make sure I don't compromise those values again.

FRIENDS

FRIENDS

I can't believe that I wrote four drafts of this book and hadn't included a chapter on friendship. Is there anything more important in your life? Even marriage is nothing more than a living relationship with your best friend and confidant. But guess what? This also requires a lot of work, just like a marriage or a partnership. The first thing to learn is that you have to initiate. You have to put yourself at emotional risk and make an introduction. You have to take the first step. Waiting for someone to talk to you or to call you will just lead to a lonely life.

If nothing else, I can say that I have tried to initiate and maintain friendships. I'm proud to say that I have friends that I am active with from elementary school, high school, college, work and the neighborhood. I call or email my friends with some regularity. I plan events, trips, golf outings, whatever it takes to maintain this part of my life.

There is one such initiation that makes me especially proud. Over 25 years ago, our sons were attending the local Catholic elementary school. We, as did most parents, participated in numerous school events to either raise money or school spirit. We always met with a lot of the same parents and developed some nice friendships. Some of the wives had a "card club" where once a month they would meet at a home, have lunch and play cards (playing cards was code for actually just chatting). The husbands often talked about doing something together as well. We talked about maybe renting a houseboat for a fishing trip. No one ever did anything, we just talked about it. One day my wife and I had free tickets to a sports and boat event, and in those days anything free was a help. We attended even though neither of us was interested in camping, boating or fishing. While we were walking through the displays my wife spotted a booth specializing in houseboat rentals. She said "You should check this out; you are always talking about doing that with your friends". I was shocked she suggested it and she probably regrets it now.

I got all the information and got my friends signed on for our first houseboat adventure.

We went to Lake Berryessa in Northern California and planned it for a late Friday night arrival and return on Sunday morning. We were still all working at that time and most couldn't take Friday off of work. The boat was a nightmare. It broke down constantly and there was no Marina. The boat had to be loaded by climbing down a muddy slope. We had enough supplies to feed a small third world country. Luckily we had an electrician and a PG&E employee with us who could repair anything. We fished (caught nothing), played cards, ate well and drank heartily. We had a fantastic time. The first night as we were getting into our sleeping bags one of the guys said "Good night Johnny Bob, good night Denny Bob, etc." It was a parody on the ending of the TV show The Waltons. It got a good laugh and we now had a name for our group. We became the Bob Brothers.

90

It is now 25 years later and next year we will be celebrating our 26th houseboat trip. The trip has expanded to a Thursday morning to Sunday morning program. You wives know that given the opportunity husbands will do this every time. The Bob Brothers each have a responsibility on the boat and mine is to plan the trip each year and keep track of expenses. The wives are very close friends as well and they get together for dinner when we are gone. They are all thankful that we never invite them on our annual trip.

It doesn't stop there. We now play golf on the trip and often during the year (our golf prowess is similar to that of our fishing). We try to get together for dinner every few months.

We attend the graduations and marriages for our families and, unfortunately, the funerals. We have lost two Bob Brothers in the last few years. However, we have added to the group as well; it keeps everything alive and positive.

The whole thing started with someone taking the first step. We have at least nine families who are happy to have such great friendships. I am so proud to be called "Denny Bob" and a founding member of the Bob Brothers.

GOLF

GOLF

What a terrible game. It is killing me. I love it!

I wished that I had taken the game up early in my life.
It is definitely a difficult sport to learn and to achieve
some level of success at when you start playing in your
middle age years. Earlier we had talked about the
importance of patience. I am not good at that and it
shows up "big time" in golf. Frustration, anger and
impatience leads to a quicker and deeper decline in
your game.

Don't do it like me. Be smart and start this game early.
Take lessons and learn the proper grip and swing. A
"don't worry" attitude will help your game immensely.
Golf comes much easier to those who are not trying to
catch up from the last shot and who are anxious to
catch their opponent. Keep it a fun thing you do with
friends. This is all good advice. I should take it to
heart some day.

They say the definition of insanity is doing the same
thing over and over and expecting a different outcome.
That perfectly explains my golf swing.

I'm not sure which I enjoy more, the golf or driving the
golf cart. I almost always drive the cart; probably since

I show up early, always put my bag behind the driver's seat and it has become just the way it is. My friends, however, often comment on their dread of riding with me. I have been known to drive a little fast and I like to get as close to the ball as possible to limit the amount of walking and exercise necessary. One such time we were playing a hilly course. My shot had gone wide of the fairway and headed for a stream (not the first such experience for me). The stream was at the bottom of a small hill and the grass was wet from morning dew. I came over the hill a little too quickly and my son was yelling "don't turn the wheel"! Of course, I knew you can't stop if you don't apply the brakes so I hit them hard and turned right. We did a 180 degree turn and slid backwards into the stream with our golf bags half covered in water. My son was yelling and jumping out of the cart. One of my friends in the other cart had seen us slide in and was yelling "they're in, they're in" and started running toward us. No one was hurt and we all pulled the cart out of the water. After we emptied our bags of water, mud, and moss, we drove onto the next shot trailing water plants behind the cart. Needless to say, it has become something difficult to live down and the story seems to grow with each telling. They shouldn't have put the creek at the base of the hill anyway.

I was just about done with this book when I had another "cart" experience. We had just finished a "shotgun" start golf tournament on the 14th hole. We had to drive back to the clubhouse and our golf cart died. This was our second cart of the day. The club had had a power failure the night before and the carts had not received a full charge. Some friends came up and we had them push us for awhile. The cart started up again and we were under our own power again. When we were about 300 yards from the clubhouse on the 18th fairway the cart died again. This time, however, smoke started flowing up between my legs and behind my back. I got off the cart and lifted off the seat cushion. There were flames two feet high! The batteries and the underneath of the seat were on fire. I started beating the flames with my golf sweater and put the fire out. A friend came up and drove us the remainder of the way back to the clubhouse. We were greeted with yells about the fairway being on fire! The entire golf cart had become engulfed in flames 7-8 feet high with a tower of black smoke. The cart was completely totaled. I had succeeded in destroying a golf cart.

Sometimes the best times have nothing to do with your golf play.

WORK

WORK

When we are in college we can't wait until we can get to the "real" world. It doesn't take long in that world to know we should have stayed in college for as long as we could have. Life in our late teens and early twenties was the best, we just never knew it.

The corporate world is not easy. The competition both internal and external can be very intense. We put all sorts of pressures on ourselves. When I was at Wells Fargo I was working hard to get a Senior Vice President title. Every couple of months when promotions were announced I was a "basket case". I would get angry that I was passed over again. Race and gender promotions were getting in my way (by the way, they were well deserved and way too late), and I kept making excuses for myself. It ate at me the whole time. I had all the responsibilities and the compensation, but not the title. I never got that title. I look back now, and I think how stupid and silly. It was so unimportant. I wasted immense amounts of energy and put untold stress upon myself and my wife for nothing.

This is not to say that we shouldn't strive to get ahead, not at all, just the opposite. Just make sure your goals are worthwhile. Building a network and a reputation as someone who can do anything is a much more valued goal. In fact, one of the values everyone should embrace is "do more than is asked". Always go "that extra mile". This reminds me of a great story.

My nephew had just started in his career and was working for a firm that was contracted by Levi Straus. A Levi executive had an urgent package that had to go out FedEx that day. She was told by the mailroom that she had missed their last pick up and nothing could be done. My nephew was in her office at the time working on her PC and offered to walk it down to Market Street (probably about a mile away) to the FedEx office there and get the package out for her. This was outside of his job scope, outside of his department's area of responsibility, but he knew he could solve the problem. He took the package and got it to FedEx in time to go out that evening. The next day his boss had already heard about the "great thing" he had done. The Levi executive bought him a Starbucks gift card as a thank you, and more important, his reputation for getting things done was enhanced.

Too often at work, we are surrounded by "negative brainstorming". We are faced with a very difficult task or schedule and we meet to plan out the project. There always seems to be a good number of people present that will insist upon coming up with all the reasons why the project won't work, we can't get it done on time, that it is stupid to do it this way, etc. I call these folks "negative brainstormers". Certainly obstacles have to be identified, but your focus always has to be on how we can achieve it or how we can achieve the largest part of the project on time and under budget. If you can rise above the temptation to focus on the negative and focus on achieving something you will succeed in most of what you attempt. You just will. Be positive.
102

Speaking of budgets, if you are in corporate life for any period of time, you will be required to prepare a budget and be evaluated against it. In budgeting, the day is won or lost when you prepare the budget, not in the twelve months following it. You should focus on "selling" your budget, and you WILL have to sell it to someone. Never be aggressive in a budget. Believe me you will be praised for making your budget, no matter how easy it was. You will also be amazed at how quickly your manager will forget how aggressive your budget was when you fail to achieve it.

The corporate world is always flush with rumors. There is constant gossiping and rumors about the next promotion, the next termination, the next office affair, and anything else that might make someone blush with interest. Here is a piece of advice that will go a long way. "Keep your head down and your mouth shut". More jobs and promotions have been lost by those who could not keep a confidence than by those that are incompetent. Engaging in rumors can do you no good. Just disengage yourself and move on. You will find out about everything that is important in due time.

CAREER

CAREER

Mistakes in career decisions can be many. Sometimes it can be funny how things work out. Your career planning does not start when you begin your first job. It starts when you sit down with your college counselor and they ask you "what do you want to major in?"

You are 18 years old and you have absolutely no idea "what you want to do when you grow up". Two months earlier you were playing basketball, playing Pedro and drinking as much beer as you possibly could. You were saving to buy that first car, the one that looks great and only needs repairs every other week, but has a great sound with its 18 speaker system.

I had a great answer. "I've always been good at math, so I'll take Accounting. That way if I can't get work, I can always do bookkeeping for companies". What a plan! It was about a 10 on the naïve scale. Of course, what do you expect for a plan that was developed "on the spot"? What I lacked in introspection I made up for in drive. I always found a way to get things done.

I took a job during school working at a women's shoe store. I was a stock boy and worked in more dust than the Sahara Desert. I was offered a promotion to sales clerk. I noticed that the sales clerks had to wear ties and had to get a size 6 shoe on a woman's foot that looked like it needed at least a size 10. I didn't think I had the physical strength for the job.

A friend of mine had a job at Wells Fargo Bank. They were flexible with his hours, paid 25 cents an hour more, and even had an employee discounted cafeteria on site (those days are long gone).

After graduation, I worked full time with Wells Fargo. I remember on one occasion they had hired someone to do the same type of work I was doing and paid them $25 dollars a month more than I. I looked for a new job and changed employers for $50 a month more. That started a pattern. I ended up changing jobs about every two or three years. In fact, I think I went through a job change both times my wife was pregnant.

Eventually, I came back to Wells and worked in a number of areas (best thing that ever happened) and went on to work for real estate firms, other banks, a logistics company and, eventually, started a Human Resource consulting company with a business partner.

My mistake in these many job changes and career decisions was that I never planned anything. It was always something that came up and I accepted it. I never made a decision to be in banking, never made a decision to get into real estate management, and certainly, never expected to own my own company. Did it work out well? Yes, in hindsight, each experience provided added employer value to my resume. That has served me well each step of the way. However, it would have made some sense to have a little direction in my career and to have given some thought as to what I liked to do or wanted to achieve.

I got some very good advice from my current business partner when he was my manager. "The bank is not going to be responsible for your career planning. They are not going to take it upon themselves to make sure you position yourself for the future". He advised often that the way you build your value in the market place is to add credentials and experience to your resume. The best job security was to be extremely marketable.

How did I put this concept into practice? I worked on my MBA while working at the bank (they actually paid for the cost), then got my real estate brokers license, and then followed that with an insurance brokers license. All of these steps, made me more marketable and the two licenses gave me the opportunity to have a little, "on the side", income.

The lesson here is to NEVER stop adding to your resume. Continually take advantage of educational or career assistance opportunities. Remember there are very few companies offering life time employment any more. You need to make yourself marketable and you need to continually build on it. Take some time wherever you are in your career to do a little planning for the next step.

Before you attend college talk to some parents of friends and learn about different industries and occupations. Not just the compensation opportunities but the work environments. Give some thought to the travel, time demands, the industry prospects, the opportunities for growth and numerous other issues.

NETWORKING

NETWORKING

Next to constantly improving your resume and your credentials, networking is the most important thing you can do for your long term success. On second thought it is more important than improving your resume. Jobs, especially as you move up in compensation and responsibility levels, are not found by emailing nice looking resumes, no matter how impressive. Positions are found through referrals and networking. Companies want to hire people they know or people who have a reputation that can be verified.

Through our career, changing jobs on our own initiative or not, we make new friends and new associations. Most of our old relationships just slip away over time. However, when we need to do a job search, we need as many people as possible to be aware that we are "in the market". Is it better to have a network of twenty or a network of two hundred?

For the last thirty years, I have worked hard to maintain a large network of business associates. Every year between Thanksgiving and Christmas I personally call over two hundred people. Past managers, peers, and subordinates are all on my list. I never ask for anything; it is not a sales call. I wish them a Happy

Holidays and ask about them and their families. It is just simply staying in touch.

In the last twenty-five years and the last four to five job changes, every change was the result of networking. When I left Wells Fargo my manager at the time was the Executive Vice President and HR Director. He told me, as he terminated me, that if he ever had his own business, he would want me to manage it. I said "Sure" and left the bank where I spent fifteen years of my life.

True to form, every year I would call him and say hello and see what was new with him. Then one time I called and he had left the bank. He was now the CAO for a logistics company. He asked me if I would do a consulting assignment for him. He wanted me to do a detailed review of his Purchasing Department. I could always use the extra money and gladly accepted the assignment. At the conclusion of the project he asked if I would consider working for him as Head of Purchasing. I declined saying "already been there and done that". He wanted to know what other functions would have to be in the mix for me to consider the position. I told him it would have to be all administrative support functions and real estate worldwide. Three months later he called and told me he now had responsibility for all the functions I had wanted and he made me an offer. I took a pay cut to make the job change to get the opportunity to get back into corporate real estate. Within two years I was making more money than I had before.

Now it really gets interesting.

After working together for three years, we decided to start our own Human Resource consulting company. This was a huge leap for me. I was not wealthy and I was just finishing paying to send three sons through college. We started the company by putting up two thousand dollars each.

It all came about because of the networking I did every year. Even more important is that it was fun every year to just call these people and see how they were. Make it part of your life, an annual event. You will not regret it.

PARTNERSHIPS

PARTNERSHIPS

When I was teaching Project Business in the eighth grade classrooms the program always included a stock market game. Each student was given a budget of $10,000 and allowed to invest and trade stocks on a daily basis. Prizes were given to the students based on overall success. I allowed the students to form partnerships with their friends. There was a method to my madness. Most soon found that their best friends were not necessarily the best person to partner with. After a few weeks, I would get students coming up and wanting to dissolve their partnerships. When I told them they would have to split the net amount the group had been reduced to there was always someone who thought they should get all their money back because they worked harder than the others. This was a great way for me to teach them about partnerships and how difficult they are to manage.

This is a great lead story about my own business. Fifteen years ago I started a Human Resource consulting business with an individual that I had worked for on two previous occasions. The first time he was actually the one who laid me off from a national bank. I had been caught up in an internal political situation and it was necessary for him to make the move while he could still provide me with some benefits.

As mentioned in the previous chapter on networking, we ended up forming a business together. Thirteen years later, we had annual revenues of two million dollars and ten employees. We sold the company for a significant profit. In 2009, we started another business together in our same building, with our same staff.

The really unbelievable part is that in all that time I can't remember a single serious disagreement between us. We live in different areas of the Bay Area; we don't socialize much together, and have very different interests. Yet, we make a great partnership. We have very complimentary skills that don't overlap much and we respect each other's expertise. It just works well.

Choose your business partner well. It is not about friendship, golfing buddies, or egos. It is about getting someone you can trust and who will trust you. Take your time with this decision since mistakes in this area are very costly; both financially and emotionally.

RESPECT

RESPECT

Treating others with respect will resolve most confrontations. It is surprising what showing a little respect can accomplish and it takes so little effort. Here is a story that illustrates how well things can work out.

In one of my corporate positions I had responsibility for corporate and facility security. We were located in downtown San Francisco in a high rise office building. I received a call one day that I was needed to assist the security personnel trying to remove a homeless person from one of our floors. The floor he was on was occupied almost entirely by women. He had been roaming the hallways asking for money and his appearance and manner were frightening the employees. The security guard was a small, unarmed woman, who was not having much luck in getting the man to vacate the building.

I brought the man to the side and asked him what he needed. I'm over six feet tall and have more than the appropriate amount of weight. He told me that he had just been released from the hospital and needed $20 to buy his medications. He even made a big deal of showing me his hospital wrist bracelet. I told him I understood but that he was scaring the employees and he needed to leave the building. I also told him if he left quietly with me that when we exited the building I would give him the $20 he needed. He was very skeptical but agreed to leave with me. When we arrived at the lobby of the building I handed him $20. He was shocked! He told me he did not believe that I would pay him. I told him "we made a deal". But I also told him if he showed up again that I would have the police called and he would receive no cash. He said "no problem, and thank you for believing me".

The story gets better.

I got called to my boss's office and he asked how I got rid of the guy. I told him and he thought I was absolutely crazy. "That guy will be back every day now". I told him, "No, we had a deal" and he laughed.

The next day I received a thank you card from all of the people on the floor where the guy had been roaming. It was signed by all the employees with notes of thanks and there were 25 one dollar bills in the card. They had heard how I had paid the homeless person and they wanted to reimburse me. My boss found out and called me. "I can't believe that you made money on this deal!"

It gets even better.

Six months later I was called down to the lobby by the security guard. Someone had left an envelope for my attention. Inside the envelope was a $20 bill, no note. I knew who had left it. It was the homeless person paying back the money.

End of story, I was $25 ahead, problem was solved and the homeless person never came back to the building again.

A little respect produced the right result and avoided a confrontation. Doesn't always work out that way but sure is nice when it does. My ex-boss still tells this story 20 years later.

DO THE RIGHT THING!

DO THE RIGHT THING!

As you move up the corporate ladder you are able to delegate the things you least like about your job. In large corporations it is likely you will experience a company wide "down sizing" at some point and you may be the one who has to deal with it. If you saw the movie "Up in the Air" you received a real look at how terminations are usually done and the impact on the person being displaced. In the movie, George Clooney is a contracted "hatchet" man. For a fee, companies hire his firm to perform the actual terminations. I never saw that done, but I had to layoff a lot of employees and it is extremely traumatic for the employee and you. The decision for a company wide "down sizing" is often made by the executive management team who does not perform any terminations. They just direct someone else to do them.

It has long been my feeling that this should be done by those who make the decisions. It is a difficult thing to do and you should not be able to distance yourself so easily from the decision to terminate someone. In other words, "Man Up" and do the tough work.

When I was with Wells Fargo I had a tough situation arise. We had a warehouse that was remote and two drivers who would do pickups and deliveries. One of the drivers brought a handgun to work and would put the gun to his coworker's head while he drove the truck. The coworker reported it to management and was too scared to go back to work.

The person managing this business unit was an elderly woman who reported directly to me. She was the sweetest person. She often offered to get me coffee or get my laundry or whatever I needed. I declined, but you could see she would do anything to please.

At this time we had been considering outsourcing the entire warehouse operation to a third party, but hadn't finalized our plans. We knew that this employee would have to be fired, but we wondered what was the right way to do it and what risk would we be exposing the coworker to. I had decided that I would fly down to Southern California and do the termination and not have my manager do this. I felt it was not right to put her in jeopardy with someone unstable enough to bring a gun to work. The strategy was to just accelerate the outsourcing of the function and terminate both employees with severance. This would at least protect the coworker from retaliation. I told my boss before I left for the trip, "If this guy comes into the building with an overcoat on (it was August and a heat wave was in effect), I'm going to promote him to Vice President".

We had planned for the meeting to take place in a secured building. The employee had been advised not to report to the warehouse but to the data center instead. A guard had been posted at the warehouse and the building locked down. At the data center we had an armed guard in the adjoining room with the blinds set so he could look in without being seen. The local HR Director was also in the adjoining room.

Immediately prior to the meeting time, I was called by the lobby and told someone asking for me had jumped the security gates and was heading up. This was not sounding good.

The employee came in the room enraged that the warehouse was closed and was yelling, "Why had I taken the coworker's side"? I explained that we hadn't done that and, in fact, considered the issue as one person's word versus another's. Further, I assured him that this incident was not being included in his file. This calmed him down somewhat and gave me time to explain to him that both he and his coworker were being laid off due to our decision to outsource the function.

He started to tell me how this was fine since he was going to become an aviation mechanic anyway. I told him we had hoped to place him in another position in the bank but clearly we couldn't compete with the challenge and excitement he would find in his aviation career. He went on to tell me how much he was looking forward to his new career. We actually shook hands and he went on his way. The HR person in the next room came in and told me she couldn't believe how the meeting had turned out and how I had turned the whole situation around.

The moral here is first to think out these things before taking the obvious approach. Second, listen to what the person is saying and jump on any opportunity to change the tone of the meeting.

The most important thing is to do the hard work yourself. Don't give the toughest job to your subordinate. It demeans you.

Here is another similar type story, though much less dramatic.

I was working at a national bank headquartered in Daly City, California. The office location was a few miles from a mass transit facility and the bank offered a free shuttle service to employees. The service was part of the operations I managed and the mailroom manager supervised the function for me. I usually arrive to work early in the morning. One morning I noticed that the shuttle was still parked in the lot and it was late enough I would have expected it to be on the road. I asked the receptionist why the shuttle wasn't on the road. She didn't know and noted that she had been getting phone calls from employees stranded at the BART station waiting for the shuttle. She had called the mailroom manager but he wasn't in yet.

I told her to give me the keys and I went to pick up the stranded employees. When I arrived at the station, the employees were angry since they had been waiting for over a half an hour. I apologized and, then, they realized that I wasn't the regular driver. In fact, a number of them knew that I was the First Vice President for Support Services and asked why I was doing the driving this morning. I simply said, "You needed to be picked up and I was available".

When I returned to the bank's parking lot the regular driver was standing there not looking too eager to see me. He had over slept and had not called in. I just handed him the keys so he could make the next run.

I went to my office and did not call anyone. Eventually the mailroom manager called me when he got to work and heard the rumors that his boss had been the shuttle driver this morning. He apologized about the

132

incident and wanted to know if he had to terminate the driver. I told him "No, but make sure he knows he has to call anytime he isn't going to be on time, and make sure you develop a call list so someone else can be contacted to make the drive". He assured me it would never happen again.

The moral here is that customer service is everything! You do not leave your fellow employees or customers stranded. When you promise a service you make sure that it is on time every day, no matter what happens.

In your personal life you come to decision points which can be critical for you. A decision that can have a long reaching impact and can be something you think of often. I had such an experience.

I was about 19 and still in college. My younger brother was 17 and was planning to get married. I had often seen myself as my brother's protector, though not sure he saw it that way. I thought it was a horrible decision. He was way too young and this would change his life. I insisted that he rethink his decision. I eventually refused to attend his wedding. How arrogant and immature of me!

He has been married to the same woman for over 40 years. They have three fantastic grown children and four beautiful grandchildren. I know he has forgiven me for this and we have a good relationship. However, I am haunted by my decision. There is not a week that goes by that I don't think of this and feel so bad that I had made such a poor decision.

I didn't do the Right Thing!

STEAL BIG!

STEAL BIG!

It is incredible the risks people take for the smallest gains. Two true stories illustrate this best.

While I was at Wells Fargo Bank they had property managers that had responsibility for certain geographic areas. They would work from home and would do scheduled branch visits to determine property maintenance that was needed. These individuals would contract locally with companies to do the work. The positions paid fairly well, around $80,000 in 1980 dollars. Additionally, they had a company provided vehicle and a modest expense account.

One day I received a call from one of the roofing companies with a complaint that they were tired of paying a certain property manager to be awarded the bid for the work. The last demand was for four new tires for his personal vehicle. An investigation was done and the property manager with over 20 years of service with the bank was fired. He lost a comfortable job for a set of tires. This was a very bad trade.

In another incident, I had a forms manager working for me that was arrogant and very difficult to work with. I frequently received feedback on him that was not complimentary. He was a minority and was not shy about reminding everyone how few minorities were in management positions in the bank. On this issue he was right. I knew it would be a long and difficult process to remove this person from his position.

Following a business trip of a few days, this individual submitted an expense account. All of the meal expenses were supported with small handwritten stubs from the restaurant tickets; all from the same restaurant. I thought it strange that a credit card was never used and that he always went to the same place. I called the restaurant and asked them to send me the detailed backup for each meal stub number. This person had added $25 to $50 to every meal he purchased. He had falsified his expense report. Internal Audit was called in and he was terminated the next day, without severance.

The moral of the story is don't steal; but if you do, make sure it is enough to live on for a very long time.

DON'T WORRY ATTITUDE

DON'T WORRY ATTITUDE

When you first learn to play golf you are constantly told to swing "EASY". You listen for awhile and before you know it you are actually hitting the ball pretty decent. So what happens then? The first thing you think is, "If I hit the ball that far by swinging easy, think how far it will go if I swing hard". The answer, of course, is nowhere since your entire swing breaks down.

A friend of mine recently returned to playing golf after an eight year layoff. He came back just for something to do during retirement. He no longer cared what his score was, how far he hit it, or if he beat the other guys. Guess what? He is playing better golf now than ever before because he just doesn't worry about his score.

Sometimes this type of attitude is exactly what you need. I have found that when I stopped struggling for corporate titles and didn't focus on financial success so much, that some things just got easier. You deal more from strength and character and you are more credible when you really aren't worried or anxious about making the deal. For example, when you can tell a client that you really don't need them because you don't like the way they do business, you send a very strong message. The client can see that you mean it and sometimes it can motivate change.

When you take this don't worry attitude to your relationships it seems to work there too. If you are insistent on making all the decisions, planning everything, winning every argument you continually are in a stressed environment.

When you can say, "I don't care, what would you like to do?" Your life gets so much easier.

Take it easy. Work will be there tomorrow. The less you worry about things, the more you will enjoy everything.

INVESTING

INVESTING

I wish I had the secret to successful investment strategies that I could just pass along to you that would guarantee you fantastic stock market and real estate gains. I clearly don't have any methodology to share. However, I have certainly made my share of errors in this area to qualify me to at least share my mistakes so maybe you won't repeat them.

In my early years, I never had any money to invest so it wasn't much of an issue for me. Buying a home in the San Francisco Bay Area, sending three children to Catholic schools and colleges, having two cars that actually ran and having a modest family vacation annually didn't leave any discretionary funds for investment. Obviously, for us, and for most Americans, buying a home should be the first priority. The tax laws that benefit us with interest and real estate tax deductions effectively subsidize our most basic investment. Additionally, we actually are able to live in our investment and we leverage our investment with the bank's money. This is a combination of factors very tough to beat.

Finally, I had accumulated enough money to invest something. I had a close friend who had a much larger net worth than I and he was willing to share his stock broker with me, someone who worked exclusively with very wealthy clients. This broker introduced me to margin trading where I could leverage my meager savings account and trade stocks at a much greater volume. In the first year I traded, bought and sold, over $2,000,000 in securities with my little savings. I made multiple trades each day. I was about $30,000 ahead on a net basis. I was, however, constantly stressed out and not sleeping well at all. I was also spending hours a day on the phone discussing trades. Then reality finally came crashing down on me. The stock market crash of October took me out. I was holding Seagate stock long and the market was dropping fast. I made a quick decision to get out of the stock market at that point, take my loss and walk away from this life style. I lost all my previous gains and about $15,000 of my original savings. I promised my wife I would no longer invest in the stock market in individual securities. It was a very tough lesson, but those are the kind you learn from. I was lucky to learn it when I was young. Since then I have limited myself to mutual fund investing in my 401K fund using a conservative investment counselor.

The lesson:

DO NOT INVEST MONEY IN STOCK THAT YOU CAN NOT AFFORD TO LOSE.

Our neighborhood was a modest working class area. Our friends were families from our Parish. I was the accountant of the group. I've had the occasion where a few of my friends have asked me to invest their money for them. This is a very complimentary request. They expressed their trust in me and one even said. "I don't know anyone smarter than you". I told him that he definitely needed to expand upon his circle of friends if that was true.

In all cases, I declined and referred them to my investment advisor. I also gave them one bit of advice. Diversify, diversify and diversify. When you start to get a little older you do not have the life expectancy to ride out the dips in the market. You need to make sure you have enough diversity in your portfolio so that no one sector will create too much of a loss of your principal.

Even my sons suffered through my errors in investing. My oldest son was thinking about buying a condo in the Mission District of San Francisco. I told him that a condo in that market would be difficult to sell in the future. He let the opportunity go.

His brother a few years later asked my opinion about buying a condo in Fremont. I thought it was a great idea and encouraged him to do it.

You know the result. The condo in San Francisco doubled in value and the condo in Fremont, thanks to the real estate crash, is worth about half of what it was at purchase.

Retirees on a fixed income fall prey to a particular risk. If interest rates drop or if inflation is on the rise there is a need for the retiree to increase their cash flow. The first solution is often moving their investments from conservative interest based securities to something that would provide a greater return. Chasing returns is a sure way to lose your money. As your returns are increased so are your risks. It is probably a better strategy to get a part-time job doing something you enjoy. This will give you increased cash flow and something to do.

RETIREMENT

RETIREMENT

We seem to always look forward to retirement and we are always worrying that we won't have enough money. The worst thing is to outlive your money. Now with Social Security, "crying the blues", our retirement benefits keep getting pushed farther and farther away.

It seems like I am never going to catch the senior discount. You go to the movie hoping to finally receive the senior discount because last week you turned fifty-five. Then you are told the discount eligibility has been moved to sixty years old. I'm sure in a few years when I turn sixty-five it will be moved again to seventy.

One thing is clear though, you need to do some serious planning before you elect to retire. Health benefits are becoming increasingly difficult to obtain once are past the age of fifty. If you have benefits through your employer you will be able to extend those through COBRA for 18 months in most states and 36 months in California. For those of us over the age of 50 this can be as much or more than $2,000 per month for a husband and wife. This is a pretty deep cut into your retirement income. If you don't have benefits that you can extend, don't be surprised to find that few insurance companies will provide you with a quote. You have to carefully plan how you will extend your benefits to Medicare age before you make the retirement decision. I thought I had it all figured out. During the writing of this book, we were terminated as clients of the PEO firm we were getting our benefits from. They gave us a 30 day notice and advised us they were not required to offer us Cobra. We went out on our own and tried to get benefits for our five employee firm. The cost for my wife and I at age 61 was $3,200 per month! This is a staggering amount. Luckily, we were able to find another PEO which would bring us on as a client. Our benefits cost dropped to $950 for both of us combined, and people still say that the health care system isn't broken.

In the last section, we discussed the tendency for retirees to increase their monthly cash flow by increasing their investment risk. In most cases, this was necessary due to a lack of planning before retirement. You have to include in your assumptions some type of inflation factor that will decrease your spending power each and every year.

Almost as important as the above is the very basic question of "what do you plan to do when you retire?" I am amazed at how many people tell me they don't have any specific plans but they have a long list of chores they want to get to that will keep them busy. That list was long when you worked five days a week, and had weekends planned around friends and the grandchildren. The list disappears pretty quickly when you are working on it five days a week. Then what will you do? I think it is important to have some specific plans for how you are going to spend your time. Travel plans, volunteering your time to a favorite cause, a part-time job, going back to school to take classes in things you've always wanted to learn about, playing golf, helping your children by babysitting the grandchildren are all good ways to allot some of your time.

Give this some thought before you leave your job, otherwise you may find yourself missing the interaction you had at work and the feeling of being needed and contributing. It is funny how poor health often finds the person who is no longer active and has "nothing to do".

NOT TOO BAD!

NOT TOO BAD!

I have lived a blessed life, with a very humble beginning and a modest end. I have a loving wife of 40+ years, three sons who I am immensely proud of, two beautiful and loving grandchildren and a large cadre of friends that I share things with. Really it just doesn't get any better than this. I am, however, still waiting for that "Hole in one".

I hope your life is as rewarding and without some of the bumps I have endured. Maybe this book will be a resource you can refer to once in awhile, when you are too angry to talk with your spouse, parents, or children and you just need some advice from, "A Regular Guy".

APPENDIX: CHARITIES

One Box For Hope, Inc.

In this book I have focused on a few excellent charities. Please support them in any way you can. You are able to make a difference:

Autism Speaks
5455 Wilshire Boulevard
Suite 2250
Los Angeles, CA 90036
Phone: (323) 549-0500
Fax: (323) 549-0547
contactus@autismspeaks.org
www.autismspeaks.org

California Autism Foundation
4075 Lakeside Drive
Richmond, CA 94806
(510) 758-0433
fax: (510) 758-1040
caf@calautism.org
www.calautism.org

PFLAG
PO Box 2718
Sunnyvale, CA 95087
pflag-info@pflagsanjose.org
www.pflagsanjose.org

Diabetes Foundation Inc.
13 Sunflower Ave.
Paramus, NJ 07652
201-444-0337
www.diabetesfoundationinc.org

One Box For Hope, Inc.
www.oneboxforhope.webs.com